...之女，宿植德本，眾人愛敬。無盡意！觀世音菩薩有如是力。若有眾生恭敬禮拜觀世音菩薩，福不唐捐。是故眾生皆應受持觀世音菩薩名號。

無盡意！若有人受持六十二億恒河沙菩薩名字，復盡形供養飲食、衣服、臥具、醫藥，於汝意云何？是善男子、善女人功德多不？

無盡意言：甚多，世尊！

佛言：若復有人受持觀世音菩薩名號，乃至一時禮拜供養，是二人福正等無異，於百千萬億劫不可窮盡。

無盡意！受持觀世音菩薩名號，得如是無量無邊福德之利。

無盡意菩薩白佛言：世尊！觀世音菩薩云何

BE A LIGHT
UNTO YOURSELF

Discovering and Accepting Who You Are from the Words of the Buddha

Design by Kristen Garneau

Library of Congress Cataloging-in-Publication Data
Tipitaka. Suttapitaka. Khuddakanikaya. Dhammapada. English. Selections.
    Be a light unto yourself : discovering and accepting who you are from the words of the Buddha / interpreted by Priya Hemenway and Philip Dunn.
        p. cm.
    ISBN: 0-7407-3821-6
    I. Hemenway, Priya. II. Lorie, Peter. III. Title.

BQ1372.E5H46 2003
294.3′82322—dc21

                                    2003045249

BE A LIGHT
UNTO YOURSELF

Discovering and Accepting Who You Are from the Words of the Buddha

INTERPRETED BY

PRIYA HEMENWAY AND PHILIP DUNN

**Andrews McMeel
Publishing**

Kansas City

CONTENTS

INTRODUCTION

B E A LIGHT UNTO YOURSELF. This was the final message of Gautama Buddha before he closed his eyes and dissolved into existence two thousand five hundred years ago. It is an eternal and simple message, a message that has inspired a myriad of seekers to turn within and to search for the experience by which they too would come to know who and what they really are.

Discover for yourself the truth of who you are, for this alone will set you free. You are the light, said Gautama Buddha. You are the very heaven you seek. All you need to do is to turn and look within. "Be a light unto yourself."

For forty years after his enlightenment, Gautama Buddha traveled from village to village in India gathering crowds of people to listen to him. In silence they would sit, with open hearts, and through the deepening silence, Buddha imparted his essential message. A few words at a time his wonderful teachings would reach the ears of those who listened.

This small book is filled with simple phrases and truths containing profound implications. They are the words of the Buddha as his disciples remembered them, for none of what he said was written down. It was some time after his death that they began to gather together the great sermons and stories he delivered, and the advice he had given to anyone who could hear. All that they remembered the disciples put into verse and committed to memory. The verses were chanted and were thus passed on by word of mouth for hundreds of years.

Eventually these sacred teachings were put into writing. The words of Gautama Buddha spread to other lands and were translated into many different tongues. They touched the hearts of thousands of people to whom they brought new understanding. The fire of Buddha's teachings kindled a spiritual revolution that is as inspiring for seekers today as it was to those who listened to him twenty-five hundred years ago. The simple truths that guide our lives, he said, can be perceived by everyone.

Be a light unto yourself. Discover for yourself the true nature of who you are.

GAUTAMA BUDDHA
A Spiritual Revolution

Gautama Buddha is the founder of what we know of as Buddhism, a spiritual tradition that is recognized throughout the world as one of compassion, peace, and understanding. With his passing, the disciples of Gautama Buddha witnessed the beginning of one of the most significant spiritual revolutions the world has known, for the great relevance of Buddha is that he took religion out of the hands of the priests and gave it back to man.

In the sixth century B.C.E., India was in tremendous upheaval. The rumble of discontent was loud and the voices of many great teachers emerged. Wandering about the country, as Buddha did, they spoke of new possibilities, new systems, new things to try.

The problem was at its root a religious one. The ways and the profound teachings of ancient sages had, over many centuries, become the exclusive property of Brahmin priests. Protected by birth in a social scheme that gave them ultimate power, these priests controlled the lives of the people of the land. They alone could interpret the ancient Sanskrit sutras, they alone could perform the costly rituals that pertained to all aspects of life, they alone could determine the righteousness or guilt of those who were inextricably bound into this tightly knit structure.

Originally designed to protect its people, the system by which the huge population of India lived divided them by birth into different classes. Movement within this social-religious structure was determined by belief in, and strict adherence to, accepted rules of behavior. Deviation from these rules resulted ultimately in being cast out of the social system—a place from which, according to the priests, the possibility of salvation did not exist.

When Gautama Buddha became enlightened, his revelation was very clear. Having spent years following the advice and working with the powerful techniques of many teachers, he finally realized that nothing, save his own direct experience, could bring him the salvation he longed for. This experience, said Gautama, is the birthright of us all.

As huge crowds began to gather around him to hear him talk about a new religious freedom, Guatama spoke the words that were to free not only those who were present at the time, but words that would be carried into foreign countries and future generations. His words have inspired thousands to seek their own awakening and to discover for themselves the truths that lie within.

The story of the birth of Gautama Buddha has been told many times. Part fact, part myth, it is a beautiful story and it indicates the great reverence with which this extraordinary being has always been held.

Suddhodana Gautama was leader of the Shakya clan and lived in the foothills of the Himalayas. He was old and had been waiting many years for a child. His wife, Mahamaya, awoke one night from an extraordinary dream in which she was transported to a shimmering mountain lake where she was bathed by four women. After dressing her they carried her to a golden mansion and lay her upon a couch. Then, while a star blazed brightly in the sky, a great white elephant was seen approaching from the north. The magnificent beast plucked a white lotus with his silvery trunk and entered the mansion. He circled Mahamaya's couch three times, touched her on her right side and disappeared, mysteriously entering her womb.

When Mahamaya awoke she knew she was with child. She told Suddhodana about her dream and he called for the Brahmin priests who were versed in the interpretation of dreams. They told Suddhodana that a son would be born to him who would have the thirty-two major marks and eighty minor marks of a great being. If this child pursued a worldly life he would become a world leader. If he turned to spirituality he would become a completely enlightened Buddha.

As the time of birth approached Mahamaya traveled to the city of her family, for it was the custom at that time for a mother to give birth in her family home. While resting for a while in the Lumbini Gardens, which were on the way, she stopped to admire some flowering trees. Raising her arm to pick a branch of one of them, she felt her labor pains begin and so she stopped under the tree and gave birth to a boy.

It is said that as the child touched the earth he took seven steps, looked in four directions and smiled knowingly. The feeling in the air was unquestionable. Something wonderful had happened. Without continuing her journey Mahamaya and her newborn child turned back and went home.

A few days later, Suddhodana was holding the babe in his arms when Asita, one of the great seers of the land, approached. He asked Suddhodana to allow him to hold the child and taking the boy in his arms, the old sage smiled as he saw the marks of greatness on the small body. He recognized him as the child that

the sages of many ages had prophesied would come, and bowed to him in deep reverence.

Suddenly, huge tears of sadness began to roll down the face of Asita. Suddhodana was taken aback.

"Why do you shed tears and sigh? Is some misfortune in store?"

"No, no misfortune is to befall the child. He is most extraordinary. If he remains in your house, he will become a ruler of all the world. If he leaves you and renounces the world, he will become a great Tathagata, a fully enlightened Buddha, a teacher of all men."

"Then why do you weep?"

"I am old, Suddhodana, and I will not live to meet him. He will turn the Wheel of Dhamma which has not been turned for countless ages. He will take innumerable beings across the ocean of birth and death to the other shore and establish them there. He will preach the truth that leads to peace. And I will not live to hear him."

The old sage Asita was right. The remarkable child became a great Buddha. The Wheel of Dhamma was turned and a wonderful new teaching was set in motion by Gautama.

Thousands crossed over to the shore of immortality. Thousands have taken the message of Buddha to heart. Thousands of meditators over thousands of years have found their way home to who and what they really are and these thousands continue to give thanks for the presence of this great Buddha.

THE DHAMMAPADA

When the words of Gautama Buddha were gathered together, a special collection was made, which is called the Dhammapada or the Way of Truth. It contains the essence of Buddha's teachings and has been treasured for centuries.

The Dhammapada is composed of four hundred short phrases that Buddha spoke directly to individual disciples on three

hundred different occasions. These short phrases were made
into verses and grouped into twenty-six chapters according to
their subject.

The verses of the Dhammapada are profound truths that were
remembered by his disciples for their simple beauty and for
their relevance to his teachings. The verses on the following
pages are taken from this book and are an introduction to the
teaching of Buddha.

Be a light unto yourself. With these words Gautama Buddha
urged his disciples to turn their attention inward and to follow
the path that would lead to awakening. He points out the
obstacles that distract the seeker and describes the joy that is
experienced by those who finally awaken to who and what
they really are.

Choice

Your life is determined by
the nature of mind.

A disturbed mind creates a miserable life.
Suffering follows this mind
like the cart behind a horse.

A silent mind creates a peaceful life.
Happiness will follow this mind
like an ever-present shadow.

Living in the confusion of a disturbed mind,
the false is mistaken for the truth
and the truth for the false.

Living in awareness with a silent mind,
you will arrive at truth
and easily recognize the false as false.

A troubled mind is like a bad roof in the rain—
the house it is trying to protect becomes flooded.
Awareness, like a good roof,
protects the home in bad weather.

Tormented by thoughts during the day,
flooded by nightmares in the night,
the mind is the cause of great suffering.

Providing silence and calm
the simple practice of meditation
gives rise to peace and tranquillity.

There are those that will recite
words of great teaching,
like a cowherd counting the cows of others.

One who practices meditation
experiences peace.
His actions are in accord with existence,
his words full of truth.

Awareness

Awareness of the present moment is the key.
Practice awareness in meditation
and experience that which does not die.

Only then will you be free.
Only then will you know abundant joy.

Watchfulness

Strive to quiet the
elusive, restless, agitated mind.

Observe your thoughts.
Observe the patterns of your thoughts
and you will see them disappear.

With the mind free of thought you will know peace.

Watch Your Thoughts

An untroubled mind
simply observes what is.

A silent mind is like a castle
that needs no defending.

Flowers

As the bee collects nectar
without injuring the flower,
so the meditator moves
through life.

The empty words of the unaware
are like flowers without scent.

The words of one who lives in awareness
are like beautiful flowers,
full of vivid color and wonderful smells.

As a garland can be fashioned
from a heap of flowers,
so compassion is created
in the meditative heart.

Unawareness

Long is the night for the sleepless.
Long is the road for the weary.
Long is the passing through endless births
for one who refuses to move toward awareness.

It is better by far to travel alone,
stumbling in the darkness,
than to travel in the company of a fool
who carries no light of awareness.

Busy yourself with thoughts of wealth,
and you will never know what lies within.

The fool who knows he is a fool, is wise.
The fool who thinks himself wise, is a real fool.

One who lacks awareness
perceives the truth
like a spoon perceives the taste of soup.

One who practices awareness,
perceives the truth,
like the tongue perceives the taste of soup.

You will become your own worst enemy
if you live without awareness.

Grow in watchfulness and meditation
and your life will be fruitful.

The Wise

If you meet one who knows
where true treasures lie
and who knows where not to look,
listen to that person.

Seek out as your companions and your guides
those who seek their own inner wealth.

As the craftsman uses tools
and carpenters work with wood,
so those who are wise work on themselves.

The wise seek the interior serenity
of a deep, smooth, still lake.

Many people run up and down the river bank
and never learn to swim.

Those who plunge into the river
not only learn to swim
but also reach the other shore.

The Master

There is no suffering
for one who carries his own light.
The master is free of darkness.

Finding joy where once there was fear,
the master is awake.

The master has no need of riches,
nothing is accumulated,
nothing desired.

Like a bird of the air
the master is free,
carrying nothing,
leaving nothing behind.

The Thousands

Better than a thousand words of wisdom
is a moment of silence.

Greater than he who conquers one thousand
times one thousand in battle,
are you when you conquer yourself.

Neither man nor god can defeat you
if you know yourself.

One day lived in meditation
is better than a hundred years of laziness.

One day lived in awareness
is better than a hundred years of misery.

One day lived in trust
is better than a hundred years of confusion.

One day lived in the present moment
is better than a hundred years of forgetfulness.

Forgetfulness

Meditate and enjoy the emptiness of your mind.
It will look for distraction.
When it wanders, call it back.

You will forget,
and your mind will lead you away from yourself.
Meditation will lead you home.

Your meditations will bring you joy
and the joys will multiply.

Forgetfulness may seem pleasurable
but it will turn to misery.

Every meditator meets forgetfulness
and struggles to overcome it.
Forgetfulness gathers in strength
if left unattended
and awareness disappears.

Just as a water pot is filled drop by drop
so one is filled by one's practice.
Whether it is remembrance or forgetfulness,
what you practice is what you will reap.

Not in the sky,
not in the deepness of the sea,
not in the rocky clefts of the mountains,
is there a spot in the world
where you can hide from yourself.

Violence

All beings tremble at an act of violence:
All fear death,
all love life;
remember this and be aware.

Disturbing the life of others will disturb your life.
Destroying life of others will destroy your life.

Encouraging the joy of others
will bring joy to your life.
Encouraging meditation in others
will bring peace to your life.

Old Age

While the world is burning
you seek delight.
Why are you not seeking a lamp
to find your way in the dark?

The brilliant chariots of kings are destroyed.
So, too, the body grows old and dies.
The only aspect of life that does not know death
is the eternal energy of awareness.

Self

If you value yourself
then watch closely.
Today and every day—
Meditate!

Don't trust the advice you give to others
unless you can use it yourself.

Only when clouds have ceased to obscure your view
will your ability to see be clear.

The World

Look upon this world as a bubble, as a mirage:
If you look upon it so,
you will look elsewhere for the real.

Look upon this world as a royal chariot;
the foolish long for it, but the wise do not touch it.

Those who have known misery,
and have found silence,
brighten up the world
like the moon that is free of clouds.

The Buddha

Having found what is eternal
the Buddha does not die
but lives in the hearts of those who seek the way
and serves as their guide.

Driven by fear,
we run away,
but from fear there is no place to hide.

Those who seek the truth,
those who seek the way,
those who seek to know themselves,
are delivered from fear.

The light of a Buddha is not easily found
and fortunate are those who can see it.

Joyful they are when the awakened appear.
Joyful they are to hear the truth
Joyful they are in their practice.

One who recognizes a Buddha,
or the disciple of a Buddha,
or the truth of a Buddha,
will find the path that leads to light.

Happiness

Let us live happily then,
not hating those who hate us!
Let us live happily then,
free from the disease of misery!
Let us live happily then,
free from the greed of the greedy!
Let us live happily then,
though we call nothing our own!

We shall be like the gods, feeding on happiness!

There is no fire like desire.
There is no weakness like hate.
There is no suffering like attachment.
There is no happiness greater than peace.
One who has tasted the sweetness of silence
has tasted that which lives forever.

One who has found the company of wisdom
has found the perfect companion.

One who walks with trust in the heart
has found the path to freedom.

One who has learned to walk with an inner light
moves like the stars in the sky.

Anger

Abandon anger, forsake pride,
overcome all bondage!
Suffering does not come to one
who calls nothing his own.

If you can govern your anger
like a charioteer his chariot,
you are a real driver;
otherwise you simply hold the reins.

There is an old saying that goes,

"They blame you if you say too much;
they blame you if you say too little;
they blame you if you say nothing at all."

In fact they blame you whatever you do.
It is only the wise who are blameless
for they are unconcerned.

Distractions

You are like a yellow leaf.
Death awaits you at the door
and you have no provisions for the journey.

Make yourself whole, work hard, be wise!
When all distractions are blown away,
you are the light
and you know the way.

Just as iron is eaten by rust
so the mind's distractions
lead you to destruction.

Unrepaired, a house falls into ruin.
Unattended, the body becomes ill.

The greatest suffering of all
is that which derives from ignorance.

Free yourself of ignorance
and you become whole.

Life is easy for those who live without shame,
who are boastful and live in corruption.
It is more difficult for those who live with integrity,
who try to be simple and calm.

Those who destroy life, who speak lies,
who take what is not theirs,
dig their own grave of self-destruction.

Know this,
that the unrestrained are in a bad state;
take care that greediness and vice
do not bring you to grief!

The faults of others are easily perceived,
and those of oneself easily avoided.
While we carefully study the faults of our neighbor,
we hide from our own.

If you find you are interested in others' faults,
be assured that your own are growing.

There is no easy path to truth.
One cannot learn it by rote.
Its way cannot be forced.
Those who arrive simply awaken.

There is no easy path to truth.
It cannot be found in the physical world,
for permanence is a dream
from which the Buddhas have awakened.

The Way

The way of the Buddha is the eightfold way.
The teaching of the Buddha speaks of four truths.
The meditation of the Buddha is to let go of desire.
The perfection of the Buddha is that he can see.

Follow the way of the Buddha as if there is no other.
Go quickly!
Be steadfast!

If you follow the way of the Buddha,
you will see the cessation of misery.

But you yourself must make the effort;
the Buddha only points the way.
The journey is yours.

If you meditate
and look where the Buddha points
you will find your way.
You will awaken.

It is through your own practice
that you will leave the world of misery.
Through meditation your mind will find silence
and you will find peace.

Cut down the whole forest,
not just a tree!
Seek out the root of misery
and you will be free.

So long as your mind is governed by desire
you will remain in bondage—
just as the calf that drinks milk
is bound to its mother.

Cut the root of desire
as you would cut back winter growth.
Take up the effort with earnestness
and learn to live with awareness.

Here I dwell
thinks the fool
not considering
the reality of death.

The flood carries away all in its path.
With the same certainty death comes
and carries off the fool
and all that he thinks is his.

Those who are more wise than the fool
recognize the meaning of this,
and make their way to freedom
with diligence.

Miscellaneous

The wise let go of small pleasures
in order to find the greater one.

One who thinks that by causing pain to others,
he will have any pleasure
is entangled in the bonds of hatred,
and will never be free.

A true seeker,
having let go of all attachment,
has destroyed the kingdom
that ruled over the land.

It is hard to renounce desire
and leave pleasure behind.
It is difficult to leave the comforts of home
and hard to take to the road.

But to cease the senseless wandering
and move onto a path with certainty
is to walk on that which will lead you away
from all that binds you to misery.

Those who meditate find their way.
They become like the snowy mountain peaks,
rising high.

Those who don't meditate
are like arrows shot at night.
They pass through life and reach nowhere.

Those who meditate
quiet the mind
and rejoice in the silence of being.

Desire

Desire grows like a creeper in the mind,
leading you to drift from life to life
like a monkey looking for fruit in the forest.

The vines of the creeper sprout prolifically.
If you see them springing up,
cut them at the root
with awareness.

Those who are slaves to their mind
float along the stream of desire,
as a spider moves upon the strands of a self-made web.

Once disentangled from the web of desire
the mind becomes free and clear.

Let go of the past,
let go of the future,
let go of all distractions from now.

If you are tossed about by doubt,
if you are full of passion and yearn for delight,
your thirst will grow
and the fetters will become strong.

If you work to quiet doubt,
if you meditate and seek the way,
you will move toward freedom
and release the bonds that tie you down.

Once you find your way—
alone and unafraid—
once you have broken the ties,
your freedom is guaranteed.

The gift of a quiet mind
is greater than all other gifts;
the flavor of this peace
exceeds everything in its sweetness;
the delight of meditation surpasses all delights;
the sensation of freedom is ecstatic.

The fields are choked by weeds,
the mind is damaged by confusion:
The practice of meditation quiets the mind
and promotes a state of silence.

The fields are choked by weeds,
the heart is damaged by hatred:
The practice of meditation opens the heart
and promotes the flowering of love.

The fields are choked by weeds,
the soul is damaged by greed:
The practice of meditation frees the soul
and promotes the wisdom of truth.

The fields are choked by weeds,
the being is damaged by lust:
The practice of meditation frees the being
and promotes the divinity of life.

The Seeker

With joy the seeker travels,
delighting in the way.
Pondering over the words of the Buddha,
the seeker remembers the teaching
and does not lose his way.

Empty the boat, seeker!
Empty the boat and ride on down the stream.
Having lightened your load
your boat will swiftly find its way to the sea.

Meditate and don't be careless,
don't let your mind wander.
Don't create the hell
in which you must cry "This is terrible"
as you burn.

There is no meditation without wisdom,
and there is no wisdom without meditation.
When one has both meditation and wisdom,
peace is at hand.

The beginning of all meditation
lies in watchfulness.
Watch over the senses,
watch the thoughts,
watch the way the body moves.

Become perfect in this watchfulness
and you will see the end of all suffering.

As the Jasmine sheds its withered flowers,
you will shed fear and hatred.

When your body, heart, and mind are quiet,
the perfect stillness is joy.

Rouse yourself,
examine yourself!
Thus attentive
you will live happily,
O traveler!

For you are the lord of the castle,
you are your own refuge;
you are the fruit that you cultivate.

All those who meditate
brighten up this world,
like the moon
brightens up the sky.

The True Master

Stop the stream!
Drive away the desires that distract you,
find the emptiness that makes you free.

Stop the stream!
Let go of the bonds that keep you restrained,
find peace in your being.

Once you are neither on this shore nor that
fearless and free, I call you the master.

By day it is the sun that shines,
by night—the moon.
The true master is one whose light
is always shining.

Desire will make you a beggar.
Longing will leave you poor.
When you follow the way,
you will live without misery,
and awake to the profound beauty of life.

ACKNOWLEDGMENTS

PAGES 6, 40, 54, 60, 82, 84, 90, 116, 118, 124, 126, 132—
British Museum, London

PAGES 10, 14, 102—
British Library, London

PAGES 18, 29, 32, 74, 76, 78, 86, 92, 112, 122, 136, 138—
Shelley & Donald Rubin Collection, New York

PAGES 21, 34, 36, 39, 66, 104, 120, 128, 134—
Art Institute of Chicago, Illinois

PAGES 22, 58, 140—
Musee Guimet, Lyon

PAGES 25, 52, 56, 130—
Metropolitan Museum of Art, New York

PAGE 26—
Franz Schertel, Passau

PAGE 31—
Eisei Bunko Foundation, Tokyo

PAGES 44, 88—
Collection of J. E. V. M. Kingado, U. S. A.

無盡意！觀世音菩薩有如是力。若有眾生恭敬禮拜觀世音菩薩，福不唐捐。是故眾生皆應受持觀世音菩薩名號。

無盡意！若有人受持六十二億恒河沙菩薩名字，復盡形供養飲食、衣服、臥具、醫藥。於汝意云何？是善男子、善女人功德多不？

無盡意言：甚多，世尊。佛言：若復有人受持觀世音菩薩名號，乃至一時禮拜供養，是二人福正等無異，於百千萬億劫不可窮盡。無盡意！受持觀世音菩薩名號，得如是無量無邊福德之利。

無盡意菩薩白佛言：世尊，觀世音菩薩云何